POETRY OF LIFE

MICHAEL F. MORTON

DEDICATION

To my Angels Three,
Michelle, Megan and Tristan

CONTENTS

Acknowledgments   i

Poetry of Life   1

ACKNOWLEDGMENTS

I would like to very much thank and acknowledge my friends and family who helped me in putting this book together. Specifically, Angela Houston, Michael Pearson, Kathleen Dokstader, and my daughter Michelle Morton. Their keen eyes helped with editing and structure of my poems. Thank you again, Michael.

1 POETRY OF LIFE

The Tree

The Tree,

The Tree,
Our sign of affinity,
Our foundation,
For all that is above and below,

We all spring from the Tree,
Interconnected by our origin,
All from one source,
The Creator of all life,

The Tree,
Where sinners and saints are one,
Each with their own branches,
And leaves yet born,

Hatred, Envy, and Anger,
Are burdens upon our tree,
Enemies of life's truth,
The most dangerous disease of the soul,

Only love can conquer the enemy of truth,
It is the only force of change,
That can penetrate the hardest heart,
And release a life of compassion and forgiveness,

The Tree teaches us to carry love for all,
To let the light of truth,
Shine through our eyes,
For love is the promise of all life,

We are all keepers of the Tree,
All given the honor and blessing to protect it,
To help others bear its fruit,
With love and compassion for all.

I this poem on 17 May 2018. This poem is about the tree of life and how all mankind is connected. I believe we all come from the same source, the same creator, God. I hope one day all mankind can see that. Read the poem again and let it speak for itself.

Music

I am in need of Music,
The fuel that feeds my soul,
A fire that never dies,
A spirit that words alone cannot reveal,

Music, an incredible force that unites,
Crossing all barriers,
The universal language,
Connecting one and all,

Music is poetry of the heart,
The energy that fills my cup,
Opening the secrets to life,
And the truth I cannot live without,

With music,
Life goes on without effort,
Those that can truly hear it,
Solitude is easily found,

Music is the magic beyond all we do,
Stronger than time,
Music holds you together,
When nothing else will,

Through music,
We wander where we will in time,
Reviving old memories,
Awakening worlds long forgotten,

When I hear music,
Life becomes crystal clear,
For music holds the secret,
And to know it can make you whole.

I wrote this poem on 19 January 2017. This poem was written for a friend and their love of music. Music is amazing, it has the power to sooth and motivate our emotions. We all have those songs, the ones that touch us like no other. They are our go to medicine, when nothing else will do. I am listening to my favorite playlist while I am putting this book together, and I hope you enjoy my writing.

Graveyard

I try to bury it deep,
So deep I cannot remember what was buried,
By my body remembers,
And the soul never forgets,

So many feelings damaged,
So many passions not expressed,
So many things left unsaid,
So many memories that will never be,

Why are they so easy to recall,
I try to forget,
I try to wash them away,
But they are forever woven into my heart,

I see through conditioned eyes,
As episodes of sorrow scar the soul,
So much time feeding the darkness,
So little time seeking the light,

I try to smile,
Forging the façade to mask the truth,
But my eyes cannot hide the pain,
Or disguise the sorrow of drowning tears,

I face the cruel monster of time alone,
As time introduces my wounds to the world,
Like ashes on the forehead,
I am marked for life,

I often visit the graveyard,
Knowing so much of me is buried there,
Some that is still alive,
Some that is still dying.

I wrote this poem on 31 May 2018. This poem is about memories, bad memories. We all have bad memories, some we have learned to make peace with, others that have a way of coming back and taking control. Some memories are so powerful, they weave into our heart and soul. There they stay, like a graveyard, haunting life forever. They say time can heal all wounds, but time is a cruel monster that doesn't play fair. Remember my friends, you are in control of your life. Asking for help is the first step, getting help is the strength to live.

Used to Be

I don't like where we are going,
Our freedoms are no longer free,
We are no longer One Nation Under God,
But we sure used to be,

We stood for what was right,
We did what we said we'd do,
We waged war on poverty,
Not people in need,

We cared about our neighbors,
Passed laws for moral reasons,
We helped build the modern world,
And never beat our own chest,

We did not scare easy,
We acted like man for all mankind,
We reached for the stars,
We sacrificed for the good of our people,

In God We Trust is now forbidden,
There is no allegiance to pledge,
We The People we used to be,
Of many we are no longer One,

We have fallen,
Given into greed,
Afraid to speak our own truth,
Respect for laws are no longer respected,

Two Hundred and Thirty Nine Years ago we made a stand,
Now is the time to stand together again,
The greatest country in the world,
We sure used to be.

I wrote this poem on 30 October 2015. This poem was about the state of our country back in 2015. The sad thing is, we are still in the same shape. I have traveled all over this world and seen places most people will never get to see. We have the greatest of everything, but we are losing it. We used to be a proud country, proud of our heritage. But now you have to be careful you don't offend others by your love of country. Flags have come down, people are burning them without understanding they are burning the very blanket of freedom they live under.

I grew up saying the pledge of allegiance in school, singing the national anthem, and bowing my head to pray. Of many we were one, and in God we trust was more than words printed on money. We spoke the truth to the world, and upheld our traditions and laws.

America made a stand at our beginning, and we will surely fall apart if we don't stand together now. I hope we can find a way to be, "We the People", we used to be.

Surface

An unsighted Life,
A life living only on the surface,
Their soul passes through everything,
And yet it touches nothing,

Why do they care more about how things look,
Then how things are,
Always willing to take the shortcut,
Missing all the wisdom beyond the skin,

Are you afraid to see what really exits on the other side,
What's behind your blinds,
If your eyes and ears are filled with illusions,
You will never witness the miracles bestowed upon you,

A beautiful heart,
Their light shines through their eyes,
A beautiful heart is not in the outward expression of the body,
But in the heart of the beholder,

Only those with truth inside,
Will recognize truth inside another,
If you only recognize that which is on the surface,
You will never get to the truth within,

Beyond the surface,
You can find treasure, in places you didn't want to search,
You can hear wisdom, in places you have never listened,
You can realize beauty, in places you fail to see,
But only if you start the journey, you didn't want to take,

Look beyond the surface,
See someone for their heart, and only their heart,
Love someone for the beauty found in their heart,
And that heart will always be beautiful to you.

I wrote this poem on 24 October 2017. I wrote this poem after seeing a woman back in 2017. I wont call it dating, because I could tell she was more concerned about looks and body type, than what was inside the heart. Well I am not a Ken doll, nor do I ever want to be. I know we are all attracted to people by their looks, and we all have our own likes and dislikes. But what if we could see more than the surface, see a person for their heart. I believe that if we can learn to see the beauty inside others, we will learn to see it in ourselves.

The Brand

From humbled beginnings,
The Hero does come,
To overcome his deficit,
He strives to quell a thirst unquenchable,

Inferior branded upon his reality,
A brand that is taken to heart,
The goodness in his qualities he cannot see,
The shroud of doubt he wears as armor,

More, more, more,
The Hero immerses himself into life,
The pursuit to fill the voids of his brand,
But none does he find,

The positive, not positive enough,
The good, not good enough he is been told,
Every achievement minimized to do better,
And in the moment, the moment is already gone,

Believing he is meant for greatness,
To accomplish more than his brand can cover,
And when the greatness arrives,
There is no pleasure in its parade,

To even the scales,
He constantly, impulsively,
Obsessively tries to more,
To be more than his brand can name,

Desperately the Hero tries to erase his brand,
A brand that only he can see,
His pursuit fuels his fire,
On this principle he validates his quest.

I wrote this poem on 16 September 2016. This poem is about me and my life. Growing up I was always shorter than everyone, always told "you're to small", "you're not good enough", "you'll never make it" etc.. Growing up in a trailer park, with not much hope of being successful, I believed it. It wasn't until my late teens did I start to question that brand and challenge myself. I took on the attitude of "OK, I'll show you".

After high school I really challenged myself, I joined the Marines. And of course everyone told me "You're too small", "You wont make it". So of course all 5'5" and 125lbs of me said "OK, I'll show you", and I did. I served 4 years in the Marines as an 0341, Infantry Mortarman.

After the Marines, I served in a law enforcement agency for a few years and proved them all wrong again. But law enforcement wasn't my true calling and so I left and joined the Army. I served 23 years in the Army and I loved it every day.

I worked hard in my Army career. I was the top graduate of every school I went to, skills training, and earned many special awards. It wasn't until I retired, I realized that even though I had proven everyone wrong, I was still wearing the brand given me as a child.

I worked hard, earned all the awards and promotions, but I never took the time to appreciate it. When the time would come for presenting the award, I was like "OK, cool, what's next"?. The achievement didn't mean much, as I was already looking to the next challenge.

Please take my advice, take the time to enjoy even the simple things in life.

Phone Calls Home

Phone Calls Home,
The longing of my soul,
The admission of my weakness,
His strength I need to endure,

Whenever I Call,
I know He will listen,
I know He understands,
And I know I am forgiven,

Phone Calls Home need not be extensive,
For only words from the heart are needed,
The message is not in the details,
But in the simple outpouring of the heart,

You can call anywhere, at any time,
When you are in need or distress,
If only to say thank you,
That will be enough,

In the silence of your heart,
The longing of the soul can be heard,
From the depths of your heart,
You will hear His word,

Phone Calls Home,
When you need to find the courage of a new day,
When you need a change in life,
You can find a change within,

When all hope is lost,
Help is only a phone call away,
When you have nowhere else to go,
You can always Call Home.

I wrote this poem on 11 August 2016. This poem is about praying and the importance of remembering to pray. Prayers don't have to be in a church, they can be anywhere. Prayers don't have to be long or complicated, as long as they are from your heart. Just remember, it doesn't matter where you are, or what you are facing in life, you can always call home.

The Smile of a Child

Have you ever realized,
The healing power,
The wealth of love and kindness,
Hidden in the smile of a child,

The smile of a child,
Where true kindness begins,
And in their laughter,
You can witness the glory of God,

The smile of a child,
A radiating fountain of delight,
An unending stream of joy,
A delight for which there is no substitute,

In the smile of a child,
You see an endless supply of sunshine and rainbows,
You lose yourself in the object of their wonder,
And unlock the treasures of your soul,

The smile of a child,
They share unconditionally,
Giving the most genuine sense of joy,
Making the brightest days brighter,

The smile of a child,
Their innocence warms your heart,
In the smile of a child,
The world can change,

In the smile of a child,
All the beauty in life,
The inspiration of our future,
A universe without limitations,

The smile of a child,
One of God's greatest blessings,
They remind us that the greatest privilege in life,
Is to love.

I wrote this poem on 26 December 2017. I wrote this poem after seeing a St. Jude commercial on TV. I was so moved seeing the children, it lifted my spirits and my day was changed. Read the poem again, take the time and see the smiles, make children smile, and your life will change.

Don't Include Me

She's got that look,
Ya she's got that style,
She's got that sassy little walk,
That always makes me smile,

Ya she's got everything she wants,
Ya she's got everything she needs,
But it don't include me,

She knows where she's goin',
She don't care where she's been,
She got all the guys chasin'
But she just calls them friend,

I tried catchn' her attention,
I tried playin' her game,
I tried to show her I was different,
But to her we're all the same,

Ya she's got everything she wants,
Ya she's got everything she needs,
But it don't include me,

So hold on Ol'e boy,
dont go beatn' your chest,
Shes a pistol packin momma,
And you'll end up like the rest,

Ya she's got everything she wants,
Ya she's got everything she needs,
But it don't include me.

I wrote this poem on 18 January 2018. I wrote this poem one night when I couldn't sleep. The words kept running through my mind, so I got up and wrote the basics down in about 5 minutes. The next morning when I was looking at what I had written, I thought it could also be a song. I shared this with some friends, and we all agreed it could be a good country song. So I wrote this with the intent of it being a song, but I will leave it to you, Song or Poem?

Two Wolves

My heart is ruled by two wolves,
One is white,
It calls me to protect the pack,
The other is black,
It beckons me unto the fight,

The black wolf is malicious and dark,
It thrives on anger, violence and revenge,
The white wolf is good and pure,
It flourishes in peace, truth and love,

Though my heart is of two,
Never mistake my silence for acceptance,
My calmness for ignorance,
Or my kindness for weakness,
For the black wolf is only sleeping, not dead

Fate whispers unto both hearts,
Telling me to be weary of the storms ahead,
But only the black wolf responds,
Bring on the storm,
I am the storm,

Some may despise the black wolf,
To which I hold no grudge,
But for those that mean to harm my pack,
Both wolves will bring a war from which there is no escape,

The spirit of the wolf lives within my soul,
Both peacefully and ferociously,
I strive to be that which I am,
Both protector and destructor,

There will always be a battle,
Between the two wolves inside,
But which wolf will rule my life,
The wolf I feed the most.

I wrote this poem on 23 January 2018. I wrote this poem after reading a story about a Native American grandfather who tells his grandson a story about life. I took that story and adapted it, but I must give credit where credit is due. No author is credited to this story, and it is believed to be a Cherokee legend.

My version is about todays warriors, the professional Soldiers, the veterans and all those who serve our country. This is also very much about my life and the two sides of my heart. One side is good and kind, the other is dark and violent. Most of the time, the white wolf rules my soul. He is good, and wants nothing more than to live in peace. The black wolf is my warrior spirit, who also wants peace. But when provoked, will be violent and ferocious in the fight. He will unleash a violence of action to eliminate the enemy, not capture, not subdue, eliminate.

I know the wolves are there, waiting for the storms to come. The white wolf tells me to be patient, to think and pray for peace. The black wolf says bring it on, this is my life. Both are eternally vigilant, both are the essence of my soul. But which wolf will rule my heart, the one I feed the most.

Mother Mary

Mother Mary
Full of love and grace,
I think about you all the time,
With that smile upon your face,

You called me your schnookems,
And tickled my toes,
You nursed my ouchies,
With a touch as delicate as a rose,

A piece of candy always ready,
Or an ice cream bar snack,
We were always ready to visit,
And always hurry back,

The simplest of crafts you made,
And all the smiles they did bring,
With a generous heart you gave,
With your creations of yarn and string,

The love you gave,
The faith you shared,
All that banded our family,
With a tender soul that cared,

I wasn't there that April day,
That God called you home on high,
As the angels sang Hallelujah,
I didn't get to say goodbye,

I am all grown up now,
With little angels of my own,
And I think of you often,
As the little piggy goes weee all the way home.

I wrote this poem on 14 April 2014. This poem was written about my Grandmother Mary. My Grandmother was an amazing woman, the patriarch of our family. I have fond memories of her from childhood till the day she was called to heaven. Grandma Mary had a candy dish in her house, and there was always a piece of candy waiting for you when you came to visit. She was an amazing seamstress, she created beautiful quilts and animals made of yarn. She never sold these items of love, they were always given to children and families from her heart.

I was stationed in Germany when my Grandmother passed that April day. I wasn't there to say goodbye, but I did make it home for the funeral service. It was a tough time, but I wanted to make sure we celebrated the way she lived, and not how she passed.

I think about my Grandmother often, and remember all the lessons she taught me in life. As a parent, when my children were little, I would play the same games with them as my Grandmother played with me. I loved making them ice cream treats and tickle their toes all the way home.

Put it on Your Heart

I didn't want to heart it,
I didn't want to believe,
But He put it on my heart,
And so too I must forgive,

My words condemned her,
I cut those ties from my life,
But my mind held on to old wounds,
And I was consumed by a heavy heart,

I wanted to forget her,
But she was always there,
For those we do not forgive,
Will always be there,

Forgiveness is letting go of your wounds,
Forgiving yourself,
Realizing that the deed is over,
Only then can we move on,

Forgiveness is an act of will,
And will can over come resistance of the heart,
For the more hurt we hold on too,
The less our wings can carry,

Forgiveness is a release of judgement,
We don't forgive someone because they deserve it,
We forgive them because they need it,
Because we need it,

Each time we forgive,
The heart of another will change,
Be it seen or unseen,
The heart will not be the same,

So put it on your heart,
Let forgiveness be your contribution to healing the world,
Forgiveness is giving,
And so to the receiving of life.

I wrote this poem on 20 February 2018. I wrote this poem about a woman who came in and out of my life for many years. I tried to make it work so many times, but we just couldn't find a way. In the end, I was blamed for all that happened between us, and I had lead her astray. Well I will never say I am not without my faults, but I truly loved her and would never hurt her in any way.

Years of a heavy heart weighed me down. I cut her out of my life completely and prayed I would never see her again. I don't remember the day it happened, but I remember a strong feeling guilt filling my heart. As much as I tried to forget her, she was always there, because I kept her there. I could not forgive her, because I could not find forgiveness within myself.

Please read the poem again and ask yourself who is weighing on your heart. When you can forgive from your heart, the heart of another will change. Forgiveness is giving, forgiveness is to receive life.

Words

Words,
What power they hold,
Once they are sealed in the mind,
They are impossible to escape,

We live and breathe by our words,
As they shape our future, or destroy or existence,
They can bring tears from the hardest hearts,
And light fires in the minds of all mankind,

Words,
Once they are spoken,
They cannot be recalled,
You can never ignore the mess they make,
Or the scars they leave behind,

You must learn the force of your words,
Or you will learn nothing,
For the limits of your words,
Will set the limits of your world,

Words are the language of the heart,
They can articulate truth and love,
But one lie,
Has the power to tarnish a thousand truths,

Words can build bridges,
Across the minds of disbelievers,
They can free the spirit,
Or imprison the mind,

The tongue is a beast to master,
For it continually strains to be set free,
If you cannot control it,
It will control your destiny,

I am the Poet,
I want to show you the power of my words,
To make you feel them, hear them,
And see life like you've never seen before.

Insert chapter one text here. Insert chapter one text here. Insert chapter

I wrote this poem on 8 February 2018. I wrote this poem simply about words and how we communicate. I think the poem speaks for itself. I am the poet, and I hope you enjoy my words.

Apple of My Eye

In my home,
There lives my dream,
His eyes glisten with innocence,
He is the Apple of my Eye,

When he smiles,
I can feel his love,
I can hear the Angles say,
Here is the Gift of Gifts for you,

From the first time I held him,
He held my heart,
The little joys he brings to me,
Have made my life complete,

At story time at night,
Or watching him climb the wall,
Those tickles, giggles, and little smiles he shares,
He is my world,

The moments he touches my hands,
Are the moments he touches my heart,
His smile does lift me up,
I am filled with love and joy,

For all of my life,
And no matter where life will take you,
You will always be,
The Apple of My Eye

I wrote this poem on 27 October 2014. This poem is about my son, and all sons.

The Fountain of Memory

The Fountain of Memory,
Lies beneath the Tree of Life,
I thirst for a drink,
But only a sip do I receive,

Smiles from the past,
Love lost over time,
I try to recall,
But I cannot find yesterday,

Dimensions of life echo,
In the hallows of my mind
Faces linger with tears of the unknown,
Firsts I cannot recall,

Illuminating memories only flicker,
As time only softens my view,
Just a glance I get,
Do my scars speak the truth,

I fear moving on,
My mind struggles to remember,
Today will be a memory,
But will I remember tomorrow,

Try as I might,
My resolve fades away,
I long to drink from the Fountain of Memory,
But only a sip do I receive.

I wrote this poem on 23 April 2013. This poem is about memory loss. During one of my combat deployments to Iraq, I sustained a Traumatic Brain Injury (TBI) from an explosion. Over time the TBI has caused many problems that I try to overcome. One symptom of my TBI is memory loss. I have lost quite a bit of my long term memory from my teens forward. Its frustrating when I talk with friends and family about events in the past, and I do not remember any of it. The memories I do have are like faded pictures. Some are out of focus and some are just blank. So I have to write things down, input them into my calendar so I don't forget. I try different techniques to remember, to take a drink from the fountain of memory. But only a sip do I receive.

MICHAEL F. MORTON

Your Turn to Sing

You held our hearts,
With arms wide open,
A legacy of love you have given us,
Your memory is our keepsake,

You taught us to love,
And how to live,
You gave us strength,
And to fight for what's worth fighting for,

God has you in His keeping now,
He came Himself to meet you,
And in His hands,
He lead you home,

Your journey has just begun,
This earth is but one we must travel,
Hope and courage He brings us,
Just by calling His name,

It's your turn to sing His song,
And join the Angels up on high,
And sing a hymn of happiness,
Sing a gift of love,

There is perfect joy and beauty,
Revealing from His everlasting light,
A ray of hope that shines as bright as the stars,
Warms our hearts with memories of you,

It's your turn to sing now Mom,
With the Angels of God's choir on high,
Singing messages of His mercy,
And whispers of His Love

I wrote this poem on 3 March 2015. I wrote this for a friend whose mother had passed away. She asked if I could write something for her to read at the memorial service. I put this in my book for one reason. We all have loved ones that have passed, and it is hard to know they are gone. But if you believe in a higher power, then it's their turn to sing with the angels. And that always makes me happy.

Karma

Is anything in life permanent,
Or are we constantly occurring,
Are we simply a work in progress,
How do you know the beginning from the end,

You can't connect the dots looking forward,
Only when you are looking back,
You must trust your path to the future,
You must believe in something,

The energy you put out in the world,
Will one day come back to meet you,
Everything we experience we must learn from,
Or you will be doomed to repeat it,

Such is our Karma,
If you believe,
How you live now,
Affects the nature of life in the future,

You get what you give,
If the good is sown,
The good will be collected,
Regardless of what we do, Karma has a hold on life

Life moves in fluid motion,
As I hold hope tenderly in my hand,
It feels like a promise,
Though I don't know what it promises me,

So is there Karma,
Or do you follow the golden rule,
Can you nurture your awareness of life,
Or simply play the fool.

I wrote this poem on 20 February 2014. This poem is simple, Karma. Always remember, Karma is a bitch. What you put out unto the world, will come back to you.

MICHAEL F. MORTON

When Your World Breaks Your Heart

What do you do,
When Your World breaks your heart,
How can you fill the empty space,
That was once your pride and joy,

It's hard to put the pieces back together,
When your dreams just don't fit the same,
And the memories you held so sacred,
Now seem out of place,

Always with me,
The stars I looked upon when times were tough,
An endless source of happiness,
A love without end,

When Your World breaks your heart,
Nothing can replace it,
A metropolis of sorrow,
The loneliness place on earth,

I won't give up,
I can't stop reaching out,
Even though it feels as if My World has,
I will hold out and keep hope alive,

Maybe one day the truth will change it all,
And the reasons will no longer matter,
The distance will forever close,
And My World will be one,

Healing is a process,
And only time can see it through,
My heart is always open to My World,
And My World will always remain in my heart

I wrote this poem on 31 July 2015. Think about what is your world. What would you do if your world broke your heart? Would you give up? I think the only thing we can do is pray that the truth will be revealed in time.

Monuments
I pause to admire the Monuments in front of me,
My wonder soars back to where I began,
Where the road most traveled I did not take,
Where the Monuments shadow pointed to the path of lesser wear,

Even though they have passed out of sight,
Their inspiration still fills my heart,
Their words still strong in my soul,
Their hand does still guide my path,

Only a special few can inspire,
Can groom the future of a new beginning,
Developing the innocent,
With counsel and respect,

Part Prophet, part Teacher,
Part Charmer, part Comedian,
Part Philosopher and Guide,
And all that is Truth,

In my memories I do recall,
The Monuments of my life,
The speakers and the thinkers,
The valor and honor they enlightened me to learn,

To not be afraid to look up and out in life,
For what's inside cannot be measured by the day,
Your path is not defined,
If you believe there are no boundaries within,

Whether we have more or less,
Does not make us more or less,
It is what we hold within,
That is our true essence,

Our Monuments will stand the test of all time,
As we edify our foundations with truth,
As we duplicate this foundation in others,
That we too, may become Monuments ourselves.

I wrote this poem on 25 November 2014. This poem is dedicated to the mentors and role models of my life. Just like monuments, their lessons have stood the test of time. I have learned from so many people in my life, but few will ever be a mentor, a monument. I hope one day, I too will have been a monument to others that have graced my life.

A Gift of Love

A Gift of Love,
That only God could give,
Has graced our lives,
So that our hearts may live,

All we have ever wanted,
Happiness cannot describe our joy,
This gift of love,
Our sweet little boy,

His little eyes upon us,
As we prepare him for bed,
A good night to Pooh,
As he bows his little head,

Our Gift of Love,
His little arms that hold us tight,
A soft gentle kiss,
As we tuck him in at night,

A Mother and Father,
Proud in every way,
In our heart's you grow,
More and more every day,

Nothing can match the innocence,
Of his trusting little face,
His heart full of love,
Spreading sunshine to every place,

A Gift of Love from God,
That Mommy and Daddy share,
Our beautiful little man,
We call Little Bear.one text here.

I wrote this poem on 2 September 2014 for one of my lifelong friends Michael and his wife Laurie. This is all about their son Little Bear and I will leave it at that.

Hero's Blood

Tribe is sacred,
An order of life,
Blood cannot be denied,
Kinship lasts through life and death,

None fight more brutally than blood,
Blood on blood,
The Tribe knows its own weaknesses,
The exact placement of the heart,

The tragedy of living with forced hatred,
Those of one blood manipulated by another,
The Hero's blood does wage the war,
A war that shall see no end,

The Hero comes in peace,
As the war has gone too far,
The thirst for blood by blood,
Dripping from the words on wrathful lips,

Given to the wind,
The affection of generations gone,
Vile words linger in shadows,
In the void of hearts and minds,

Upon the hero's back another brick,
His world does weigh,
Carrying forth the burden,
With only his two hands,

Is hell here and now,
The Hero's blood does rage,
Why doesn't faith spring forward and save him,
Or is it his penance this road to travel.

This poem was written on 3 September 2015. This poem is about family, and the wars fought within. Wars within a family are merciless. Because the tribe know the targets of the heart. Words are more damaging than daggers, for they leave scars that can last a lifetime. You may be able to survive the wars, but no one gets out unwounded.

One

On every turn,
More and more pain I find,
People with empty eyes and broken smiles,
Still searching for a tomorrow of love,

Love is not in the color of Man,
For Man is of One kind,
One of flesh and blood,
One in the Father's image we are all created,

Why do so many follow the crowd of promised lies,
Will they ever see our beginnings are as One,
Our hearts are born without the knowledge of hate,
As all hearts begin with love,

We must see through these poisonous ideologies,
And see We are all of One,
Those with haloed heads,
Their cultured deeds shall be imparted no more,

Taken is a gift from the Father,
When any Life is taken,
Love they neighbor as thyself,
As the Father commanded long ago,

There is a place where you can still find love and understanding,
A place filled with vibrant colors that shine,
Where every color is equally beautiful,
And the light of heaven encircles the soul,

Only from this place,
Will we see all of Man as One,
Just as the Father had planned,
When you see One from the Heart.

I wrote this poem on 27 July 2016. This poem is about race, and all the hatred that has evolved by color. I was raised to see people for who they are and not the color of their skin. So many are out there following blindly, practicing hatred without knowing why. Hatred is learned, you are not born with it.

Have they forgotten, we are all of One. One of the Father, one creator. And everything created by the Father is beautiful. Any life that is taken, is a gift taken from the Father.

Only from the heart, can we see everyone as One.

To Be Continued

I had no control over my beginning,
Or how my Journey will end,
My life has been mine to master,
And only God has determined the path for my soul,

No one can live my Journey,
It is mine and mine alone,
I have seen many great destinations,
But yet to see my end,

Every moment of my Journey,
I am where I am,
The Journey is not about where I have been,
But how far I have come,

I've gotten lost and found my way,
Discovered treasures and lost everything,
I have faced the fears of who I am,
And who I am not,

Pain has given me the power to heal,
And the strength to be resilient in confusion,
The wisdom to endure the future,
And the ability to see the beautiful parts of my own life,

Those I've meet along the way,
Have enlightened me with love and kindness,
As many of my destinations,
Have led to new beginnings,

There are many obstacles I've yet to face,
On this adventure of limitless possibilities,
Only the Father knows the time I have been given,
And only then will I see my Journey complete.

To Be Continued.......

I wrote this poem on 1 August 2016. This poem is about the journey of life. I will let the poem speak for itself. No matter what obstacles you face in life, keep going. Life is full of limitless possibilities, and only the Father knows our true destination.

Flower

She is a Warrior,
Yet delicate as a flower,
If only her petals you see,
Never shall you know her brilliance,

Her heart is rare,
Imbued with the spirit of life,
She sees the blessings,
Where most only see burdens,

She is a flower that blooms in the desert,
Proving to the world,
No matter how great the adversity,
She will overcome,

Rare indeed she is,
With wisdom humbled in quiet grace,
She reminds you that life is beautiful,
With gratitude that springs from within her soul,

She walks in life with purpose,
Alive with life in life,
Her eyes speak their own language,
That will one day find their answers,

She dreams as big as the sky,
As her heart sings endless songs of hope,
Her spirit soars above the worries in life,
Her essence a true gift from God,

She is a Warrior,
Yet delicate as a flower,
Rare indeed she is,
With faith seen as a beautiful flower.

This poem was written on 14 April 2017. This was written for a Soldier, a Warrior, a Lady among women. I served over 23 years in the military, and very few have earned my complete trust. Flower is one of those few, and her being woman has no bearing on that decision. She has a spirit that infuses all life around her and I am blessed to know her. A Warrior is not defined by their gender, and a flower is not expressed by its petals.

Let it Go

If you want Change,
Then you must be the force behind the change,
Be smarter than your pain,
And stronger than your fear,

This journey is not about becoming someone,
It's about un-becoming everything that isn't you,
To give as much energy to your dreams,
As you do your fears,

Every challenge you face is a lesson,
A chance to create your own future,
To master the unknown,
To find the you, you have not yet found,

Strength comes not from words,
But from your character,
Your indomitable will,
The courage to face yourself,

Change can offer growth,
Growth offers new opportunities,
Wishing for a different past,
Will only waste your present,

These walls you have built,
The invisible armor to which you cling,
Will not change your outcomes,
Until you open up and step into life,

There can be no healing,
Without pain and suffering,
There can be no moving forward,
Without letting go.

This poem was written on 7 April 2017. This poem is about letting go of all the pain and obstacles in your life. Read the poem again, think about all the things you need to let go of in life. You cannot heal if you are stuck in the past, you cannot move forward without letting go.

Right Now

Opportunity is passing you by,
Justice is being corrupted,
People are busy on their phones,
Racism still exists,
You could be outside enjoying the day,
People are dying,
Guilt is devastating someone,
People are planting bombs,
A child is going hungry,
You are reading this,
Nothing is more expensive than regret,
People are praying,
The truth is being hidden,
Someone is working for nothing,
Your family misses you,
No one is safe from loneliness,
Someone has a broken heart,
Someone is moving on with their life,
Time is leaving you behind,
It's not as hard as it looks,
Life is getting shorter,
Is happening,

What are you doing, Right Now?

I wrote this poem on 26 May 2017. I wrote this poem after watching CNN one morning, and I couldn't help but think, What am I doing right now? Am I living in the moment? Or is life passing me by? There is so much going on in the world, it can distract us from living. Think about what's going on in your life, Right Now.

When I Close My Eyes

When I close my eyes forever,
Will I have made a difference,
Did I give,
More than I received,

Was the purpose of my life to be happy,
Was I useful,
Was I honorable and compassionate,
Did I live a life well lived,

Did I do something to be someone,
Did I shake the world gently,
Did I work to change the lives of others,
Were the results of my actions worthy,

Did I do more than just care,
Did I do more than just believe,
Did I do more than just be fair,
Did I do all that I could to forgive and forget,

Did I stand with everyone,
Or did I stand out from everyone,
Did I dare to test the tides,
Or was I only treading water,

Did I share my knowledge to enlighten others,
Did I nurture the inquisitive nature of a child,
Did I show the world why I was born,
Or did the world show me,

When I close my eyes forever,
Will I be remembered for the difference I made,
Did I give more to the lives of others,
Did I live a life well lived

This poem was written on 7 June 2017. I wrote this poem about life, my life. I know I have lived a life, but have I lived a good life. Have I given more than I received. Did I make a difference in the world, or was I just a passenger along for the ride. The biggest question I ask myself, was I honorable? I believe one of the most important attributes in life is honor. If you lose your honor, it's almost impossible to get it back. Read the poem again and ask yourself, When I close my eyes forever, did I live a life well lived.

The Summer Rain

Clouds gently floating by,
I smell the rain and feel the wind,
My thoughts become alive,
As I crave that enchanted sound,

The soft pitter patter,
Silent but not empty,
The sound I yearn to hear,
A sound so worth listening to,

The rain gently falls,
Slowly filling my cup,
Bringing new hope to my rainbows,
Washing away my troubled path,

Oh the summer rain,
Kisses upon my forehead,
God's grace descending upon me,
The cleansing of my soul,

We splash around on empty streets,
My daughter and I, hand in hand,
The drops dance upon our lips,
As we laugh at our silly little show,

I am a child of heaven,
Blessed by the Father's love,
My spirit soars with happiness,
As we skip and prance around the puddles,

After the rain,
The sun will always shine,
There is peace in my life,
And in my life I find great joy.

I wrote this poem on 22 June 2017. I wrote this poem after talking with a friend, and hearing her tell me how she and her daughter love to dance in the rain. Just a simple poem about a simple pleasure in life.

What's Your Fear

What's Your Fear,
Are you afraid of being inadequate,
That your dreams are impossible to achieve,
Or that you are powerful beyond measure,

Fear has no decency,
Respects no laws or purpose,
It finds your weak spot,
And shows no mercy,

Fear keeps you focused on the past,
Or worried about the future,
Fear becomes the darkness you avoid,
And pulls you back from life,

Fear can become your heaviest burden,
And some cling to their fears stubbornly,
For once fear is gone,
They are forced to live with reality,

Liberate yourself from your fears now,
And your presence will liberate others,
Find the courage to accept your own experiences,
For fear is only as deep as the mind allows,

Face your fears,
And fear will have no power,
As fate cannot be taken away,
And you will still remain,

What's your fear,
Are you still afraid of the darkness,
Are you still afraid of the past,
Or are you afraid of dealing with the reality of your future.

I wrote this poem on 1 August 2017. I wrote this poem after talking with some friends about fears. We talked about our fears, and I was surprised to hear it wasn't about spiders or snakes. We all have fears, but why are they fearful. The simple answer is because we have given them power to be. The fear that controls us, is given control by us. Only after you take that power back, will you liberate your life. So, what's your fear?

My Journey Home

My Journey Home,
The place where open hearts are waiting,
The journey to find my smile again,
To become once again everything that is me,

Upon this journey,
I leave my sorrows behind,
I will live life on my own terms,
And never apologize for it,

I have set my goals,
I have charted my map,
And like every river that must find its way to the sea,
I too must find my way home,

Some yesterdays will still remain,
For without the memories of my beginnings past,
The greatness of my destination,
Will be lost for all time,

I have walked upon the stones of life,
And there have been setbacks, surprises, and gifts along the way,
But I have kept moving forward in my faith,
And I remember just how valuable I am,

No longer will I be trapped on the treadmill of time,
No longer will I feed my fears,
All the duels with my demons are over,
For I have embraced my own purpose and I am my priority,

I am on my way home,
To the place where open hearts are waiting,
I will find my smile again,
On a journey that leads to new beginnings

I wrote this poem on 26 July 2017. This poem was written for a dear friend who was on her journey home. Her journey wasn't just to travel back to her hometown, but back to where her smile truly belonged. Going home isn't always a simple trip. Sometimes the stones that we have collected in our shoes, weigh us down. Empty your shoes my friends, let your faith guide you home where you truly belong.

Tears of the Blind

There is so much sadness in the world,
A time when the spirit of man has been subdued,
When the past seems a storm swept desolation,
And the tears of the blind see no hope for the future,

Man has been cut off from the soul,
Cut off from life,
Contaminated by temporary happiness,
Altering the ability to give or receive life,

What is the reason for this madness,
The breakdown of society,
With millions living discontented lives,
In the depth of darkness,

Is it power and selfishness,
A consumption of desires that can never satisfied,
Running blindly into the illusion,
Of the void that can never be filled,

The more they see,
The more detached to the vanity of recklessness they become,
Left only with the shadowy nights of the soul,
And the future but a way of death,

Now is the time,
For the world must see the sadness of all humanity,
The sober eye of reason,
Must see the unsatisfied need of man's quest for power,

Nothing can cure the soul but truth,
Only when man is ready to love man,
Will man learn to love himself,
And the tears of the blind,
Will see a future for all mankind.

I wrote this poem on 1 April 2018. I wrote this poem after watching the news one day. All the violence and anger going on around the world, and those in power ignoring the truth, in order to gain more.

I wondered if blind people cry. If the blind see no hope for the future. Think about the beauty in not seeing people for their race or color. Or being so consumed with power, that the lives of others mean nothing.

I used to believe that man would evolve past racism, violence and power. But the fact is, many are just as blind to these tragedies, than people without vision. They are so detached from the truth, they believe death is just a way of life.

Read the last lines of the poem, think about the truth we are in these days. Maybe one day mankind can see, just as clearly as the blind.

Silence

It has taken me a lifetime to learn,
To sit silently and watch the world,
For silence is pure,
And silence never betrays,

Silence is of many kinds,
And breathes many meanings,
It is a blank page,
from where you can write within,

Silence is energy,
That brings all life together,
Its motion glides over you,
Without shape or form,

To hear the silence,
You must become part of the silence,
As sound is fragile,
One loud noise and it is gone,

Silence is everything within our perception,
And all that is beyond,
It is the core of our existence,
And the peace of mind within,

Listen to the stream that has no language,
Coursing beneath a quiet heaven,
Listen to the morning dawn,
And hear the world come alive as the Sun kisses the sky,

Out beyond the wondering night,
Where the soul lies in blissful sleep,
Where the light dances with shadows,
Silence reveals the instruments of our thoughts,

You must listen to the silence and learn,
Do not let your voice drown in the noise of others,
For those who do not understand your silence,
Will never understand your words.

I wrote this poem on 11 June 2018. This poem is about silence. Can you enjoy silence? Can those around you understand your silence? Read the poem again and think about your silence. Can you hear it?

Own Your Story

Everyone has a dream,
But do you have the courage to follow where it leads,
To dream your own vision,
Ignoring the expectations and opinions of others,

When you least expect it,
Life will test the limits of your will,
You cannot pretend the challenge isn't there,
For life doesn't wait for you to accept your destiny,

Success rarely comes easy,
We all stumble and fall along the way,
But only you can get up and try again,
Because the road of life I always under construction,

Courage is not always a loud roar,
Sometimes it is the quiet voice,
That tells us failure is not fatal,
And I can try again tomorrow,

You cannot be afraid to leave your pond,
Or you will never know the ocean,
Holding on to all that you know now,
May be the reason you miss all there can be tomorrow,

Confront your fears,
Drive the dark parts of your life into the light,
Be your own hero,
Never someone else's victim,

Own your story,
Embrace your vulnerabilities,
The experiences that create our worst fears,
Will empower you to explore the darkness.

I wrote this poem on 19 June 2018. This poem is simple, be yourself. Be your own hero, not someone else's victim. Read the poem again, own your story.

Mother

She is soft at the edges,
Tempered with a heart of gold,
With no limits to what she can do,
Or will endure for our family,

She is gifted,
With a love unlike any other,
Instantaneous and forgiving,
With a sympathetic voice that can calm all fears,

She will move heaven and earth for our family,
With kisses that can cure any wound,
She says "I Love You",
Without whispering a word,

She can feed our family with nothing,
And make it a gourmet meal,
With "Take it or Leave it",
Always on the menu,

She forgives and forgets,
Even when the world has turn and run,
She loves unconditionally,
Even when we least deserve it,

Because of her,
We have the greatest treasures in life,
Her love is everything,
The strongest energy in our world,

The best thing she can ever be,
Is the mother she was meant to be,
And the best gift I have ever received,
Is Victoria as my wife,
And the mother of our children.

I wrote this poem on 28 June 2018. I wrote this poem for a friend, in honor of his wife's upcoming birthday. I believe this poem talks about many mothers, wives and the wonderful life they create for us. Read the poem again, go thank your wife and mother for all they do. They deserve all the recognition in the world.

The Mountain

On my climb,
I am humbled and strengthened,
I marvel at the sun glistening on the rocks,
The leaves dancing upon the breeze,

I feel like never before,
I have time to ponder, imagine, dream,
I tire, I rejuvenate, I thirst,
I find within the eternal child,

The closer I come to the mountain,
The more it disappears,
Losing itself to itself,
Vanishing in the detail of every step,

Once I reach the top,
I am joined by the above and below,
Received by the winds of the future,
Heaven, earth, and man become one,

Going down the mountain,
I become closer to the mountain,
And the closer I get,
Its realization becomes known,

My realization comes with every breath,
The heartbeat in every step,
It lives within my bones,
And guides the passion of my soul,

The resolve of my mountain,
Time to focus on my soul,
So many have lost their way,
Journeying to the edges of the earth,
Ignoring the journey to the edge of one's self,

If you want to awaken from a slumbering life,
Put your ear to the heart,
For the voice of honesty,
Will always be clearly heard,

If you want to find the path to your mountain,
Keep your ear to the heart,
Listen to the voice,
And He will guide your soul to action.

I wrote this poem on 21 May 2018. I am not going to tell you what this poem is about. Read it a few more times and think. If you can figure out your mountain, then your journey has already begun.

This picture was taken on September 11th, 2008
At the Old Ministry of Defense, Baghdad, Iraq

ABOUT THE AUTHOR

Michael Morton is a freelance writer and Poet. He has published 5 books on poetry, the "Return to Innocence" series and has work forthcoming in Leadership, and Life Lessons for Little People, children's stories that promote values and morals . He is retired from the U.S. Army and served numerous combat tours in Iraq and Afghanistan. He is a recipient of the Purple Heart, Bronze Star Medal for Valor, and Army Commendation Medal for Valor.